Leveraging Masterminds

I0468203

Unlock Your Life's Potential
with the Missing Piece to 'The Secret'

(even if you have no experience, and no contacts)

LEON JAY

Copyright ©2016 by Leon Jay. All rights reserved.
Published by FHQ Publishing

FIRST EDITION 2016
No part of this publication may be reproduced, stored,
shared, or transmitted in any form (physical or electronic)
without prior written permission from the author.

1st ed.

ISBN-13: 978-1523887309
ISBN-10: 1523887303

Disclaimer:
All the information in this book is true and accurate to the
author's knowledge. However, he may be wrong. None of the
information is meant, nor should be taken as, legal advice.
The content is meant as inspirational and educational only.
Any advice, suggestions, or resources you choose to use, you
do so at your own risk. Every mastermind group is different,
and therefore, no specific result can be guaranteed.

For further information, please contact:
E-mail: support@fusionhq.com
Web: www.LeveragingMasterminds.com

To learn more about the author, visit: www.leonjay.info

CONTENTS

CONTENTS 3

FOREWORD 5

[1] INTRODUCTION 7

[2] WHAT IS A MASTERMIND? 13

[3] THE STAR OF SUCCESS 17

[4] USES FOR A MASTERMIND 23

[5] BENEFITS OF A MASTERMIND 33

[6] WHY MASTERMINDS FAIL 39

[7] FINDING AN EXISTING MASTERMIND 47

[8] HOW TO BE A GOOD GROUP MEMBER 53

[9] THE IMPORTANCE OF HARMONY 57

[10] CREATING A MASTERMIND 61

[11] NAMING YOUR MASTERMIND 67

[12] STRUCTURING YOUR MASTERMIND 71

[13] RECRUITING FOR A MASTERMIND 79

[14] FILTERING APPLICANTS 83

[15] CREATING ACCOUNTABILITY 85

[16] THE PIRANHA TANK METHOD 93

[17] THE FIRST SESSION 99

[18] TIPS TO RUNNING THINGS WELL 103

[19] THE FACILITATOR IS THE DETERMINING FACTOR FOR SUCCESS..109

[20] HOW TO PROFIT FROM A MASTERMIND..........115

[21] ADDING VALUE 121

[22] THE ULTIMATE MASTERMIND 127

[23] AFTERTHOUGHTS...131

APPENDIX 1: QUESTIONS TO HELP DEFINE YOUR MASTERMIND GROUP...135

APPENDIX 2: EXAMPLE OF A MASTERMIND STRUCTURE 137

APPENDIX 3: EXAMPLE RULES SHEET......................139

APPENDIX 4: EXAMPLE RECRUITMENT INVITE.........141

APPENDIX 5: SUGGESTED ACTION STEPS TO RECRUIT NEW MEMBERS...143

APPENDIX 6: EXAMPLE APPLICATION FORM 145

APPENDIX 7: STEP BY STEP GUIDE TO USING THEMASTERMIND.NZ PLATFORM 147

FOREWORD

*"If everyone is moving forward together,
then success takes care of itself."*

HENRY FORD

For years I have both taught and experienced the benefits of participating in a quality mastermind.

Over the course of this time, I have seen many lives changed, transformed even, thanks to this powerful process.

When asked to write a foreword for this book, I was initially skeptical. What could possibly be said on the subject that has not been said before?

After reading it, however, I understood its value immediately. Many of those details that you only learn through experience, yet make all the difference, have been covered in such a way that everyone from total beginner to industry veteran can understand and benefit from them.

The mystery has been unveiled, the fluff removed, and the complex made simple. This book offers essential reading for mastermind participants, organizers, and facilitators alike.

[1] INTRODUCTION

"Never doubt that a small group of thoughtful, committed citizens can change the world; indeed, it's the only thing that ever has."

MARGARET MEAD

Margret Mead may have been talking about the power of small groups in respect to activism and revolution, but it is just as true for masterminds.

Indeed, these small groups have literally caused revolutions in both the political sense and within their respective niches.

To understand how powerful a mastermind can be, let's return in time . . .

It was the early 1900s when six men from Chicago decided to form a mastermind. Each was of limited education, each had no real money to speak of, and not one had access to any substantial line of credit. Not the most promising of starts.

Yet these six men had a few things that were far more important than education or money. They had focus and determination, and they had each other.

They began to meet regularly and to support each other in their ambition to achieve financial success. Within a few short years, each had become a multimillionaire. And this was at a time when a million dollars was worth far more than it is today.

One of these men was none other than William Wrigley Jr., who founded Wrigley's chewing gum, now a global brand. Another, John D. Hertz, founded the Yellow Taxi Company.

Hertz eventually sold his taxi company and went on to buy a car rental company. This new company took his name and became another leading and internationally recognized brand.

Not too bad for a group of men whose future looked less than bright. And while their story may be impressive, they are far from alone.

Business and personal development gurus have long spoken about the power of mastermind groups. But masterminds are certainly not limited to the business world.

Many famous people throughout history have stated that masterminds were a fundamental part of their success. Some claim that it was in fact their participation in a mastermind that allowed them to reach such high levels of achievement.

These included many who were at the top of their game. People such as Andrew Carnegie, Franklin D. Roosevelt, C.S. Lewis, and Thomas Edison, to name but a few.

If you have never been part of such an elite group and wonder why you are not getting further ahead, then this may well be the missing key.

Indeed I believe this is the missing piece to the "law of attraction" as popularized in the book and movie *The Secret*.

The Secret was largely based on the work *Think and Grow Rich* by Napoleon Hill. And it was this very same author who first coined the term "master mind" in an earlier book, *The Law of Success*.

He went on to re-emphasize the importance of masterminds in *Think and Grow Rich*, but many teachers of his work have focused almost purely on the goal setting, visualization, and affirmations.

Hill, however, explained that the power of a mastermind was needed to really achieve success.

This is not to say you should not set goals or visualize or say affirmations. Just don't expect the same level or speed of result as when you apply these principles while participating in a mastermind.

If you have participated before but found your group failed to deliver, don't despair. Continue reading and all will be explained.

This book uncovers the mystery behind these groups and shows you how to join or create one.

It also teaches you how to overcome many of the pitfalls that adversely affect many masterminds and how to make existing ones more efficient and effective.

And fear not. Included throughout the book are all the information and resources you will need, no matter whether you are a total beginner or a seasoned pro.

So with that said, let us start our journey at the beginning . .

[2] WHAT IS A MASTERMIND?

"(a mastermind) consists of two or more people that work in perfect harmony for the attainment of a definite purpose."

NAPOLEON HILL

I am guessing that you already have an idea of what a mastermind is (or you probably would not be reading this book). However, I can't make this assumption for every reader. It is also good to make sure we both have the same definition and are on the same page before moving on.

No doubt there are many definitions, but in its most simple form, a mastermind is two or more people meeting together with the same or similar goals and/or purpose.

Perhaps the most common type of a mastermind is four or five people coming together on a frequent, recurring basis, with a collective focus on helping each member of the group achieve his or her own goals.

Mastermind groups usually blend the characteristics of a support group and a think tank with information sharing and accountability partnerships.

As mentioned, Napoleon Hill first talked about masterminds as far back as 1928 in his book *The Law of Success*. However, it was his 1937 book, *Think and Grow Rich*, that really popularized them.

Since then they have been taught about and adopted by many individuals, businesses, and organizations.

Even before this, though, Franklin D. Roosevelt was famous for using "Brain Trusts." These were groups of highly intelligent people that would assemble to find solutions to the country's pressing problems.

He may have used a different word to describe them, but these brain trusts were a form of mastermind group.

These days, masterminds are used by many different types of people and for many different reasons. Some are more like think tanks, some run more like support groups, others like information sharing or networking hubs.

Recently it has become quite a trend for well-known business gurus to use masterminds as a business model, charging for access to join their group. This gives members direct access to their favorite guru and helps them expand their network at the same time.

This type of group is often very expensive due to the limited spaces and may not be suitable (or available) to everyone.

Don't panic though. Many masterminds are free to join, and many are recruiting new members.

Each mastermind is different and unique in its own way. The important thing is that it meets the needs and expectations of each group member.

Throughout the following pages, you will learn how to do just this, and much more.

[3] THE STAR OF SUCCESS

"Success is nothing more than a few simple disciplines, practiced every day."

JIM ROHN

I mentioned that I believe masterminds are the missing piece to the success puzzle.

I have read literally hundreds of books on success and personal development, many of which either directly or indirectly had their foundations in *Think and Grow Rich*.

Each one has tended to focus in detail on one or two strategies for changing your life. Some focus on visualization or affirmations, others on goal setting or the importance of taking action.

And a few, like this one, focus on masterminds.

If you go back and look at the original *Think and Grow Rich* book, though, Hill spoke about the need for all these things. Few books really make this link, so to help with clarity, here is what I call the star of success . . .

In this chapter, I will give a quick outline of the importance and function of each point and how they link together. It is certainly worth researching each of the other points in more detail. Just understand that for maximum effectiveness, none stands alone.

Set Goals

To start, it is good to have a general goal. This could be to reach a particular sporting achievement, make more money, develop your relationship, create a new widget, or solve a particular social issue.

At the first stage, the goal is likely to be rather undefined and fairly generic. As you progress, though, your goals will become more targeted and defined.

Goals set direction, help plan necessary action steps, and allow you to quantify and measure progress.

Visualize

Once you have your goals, spend time visualizing them regularly. To do this you can either meditate on your goals or spend time absorbing yourself in a visualization board.

Visualization helps create clarity and maintain focus, and creates inspired ideas. From a metaphysical perspective, it also sets into motion a chain of events that will help bring about future coincidences that will assist you in achieving your goals.

It is the inspired ideas that you must especially listen to. Jack Canfield tells the story of how he was visualizing his first $100,000. Lying on his bed and staring at a picture of a fake $100,000 bill, he got the idea to sell a lot of copies of his book.

It was this inspired thought that led to a sequence of ideas and actions that eventually became the *Chicken Soup for the Soul* success.

Affirm Everything

Affirmations help change thought patterns.

It is said we have between 50,000 and 70,000 thoughts every day. The vast majority of these are subconscious. It can also be these very same thoughts that sabotage our potential success.

There are plenty of experts who believe confidence is more important than intelligence when it comes to most success. Affirmations are a tool we can use to help us grow our confidence, deal with sabotaging thought patterns, and again maintain focus.

Mastermind

The next step is to take these ideas and mastermind with other likeminded individuals.

The mastermind group will provide additional clarity, feedback, and focus to your goals. In addition to this, they provide support, encouragement, information, networks, and resources that can help in achieving success.

A mastermind will help prevent you from making unnecessary mistakes and will get you thinking at a higher level.

Virtually every significant achievement throughout history has resulted from participation in a formal or informal group. A good mastermind will leverage and magnify all the other points on the star of success.

Action

Nothing happens until something moves. Once you have direction, clarity, confidence, and support, taking action will come naturally.

Some actions will lead to mistakes. This is inevitable, and so long as you measure and learn from your results, you can adjust and try again.

It is this "action, fail, learn" feedback loop combined with clear goals, inspired ideas from visualization, confidence from affirmations, and the support and collective intelligence of your mastermind group that will lead to success.

It is possible to achieve some success while missing one or two of these points. However, each one, when used correctly, will compound on the effect from the other others and result in a much higher degree of success.

It should also be noted that while I have described the star as a circular process, each point is also connected to every other point. They link together and work together as a single unit. When used in this way, the results are much, much stronger.

Now that we better understand the way these five elements of success work together, let's master masterminds . . .

[4] USES FOR A MASTERMIND

"A mastermind group is just as much about the place you're going as it is about the people you're going there with. In other words, it is designed for a 'definite purpose,' and establishing that purpose is the first step."

TYLER WARD

Most people think of a mastermind as something for business owners, and perhaps this is indeed the most common use. However, masterminds can be used for almost any type of goal.

Here are just a few suggestions (starting with the obvious) . . .

Business

Entrepreneurs and business owners have long adopted the use of mastermind groups. However, not all use them for the same reasons or in the same way.

Many groups are made up of individual business owners that are looking to accelerate their business growth. They will typically have different types of business and meet together once every two to four weeks.

For example, one group I was in had one member with a supplements company, another with a travel clothing brand, another with an online dental directory, one that produced exercise equipment, and one that provided copywriting services, while I had a software company. We would meet every two weeks and assist each other's progress.

Because of the diversity of our businesses, we never worried about sharing secrets to the competition, and we were able to borrow expertise from a range of different industry experience and knowledge. Most importantly, we held each other accountable for our goals.

Other businesses, however, may choose to create internal mastermind groups. For example, the heads of different departments could meet every two weeks to mastermind together.

During this meeting, they can help each other overcome their challenges by bringing the brightest minds in the company together to find solutions to the most important problems.

This can be really beneficial, as it helps the departments understand each other's challenges better and work more toward the common goal of the company (instead of creating an internal us versus them attitude).

Small teams can also use masterminds as a way to advance quicker by using the collective intelligence to solve problems and by increasing focus through peer pressure and group accountability.

Investing

Investors can also benefit from joining a good mastermind group.

By sharing their challenges and objectives, members can help each other reach their investment goals.

This may be via sharing contacts, investment opportunities, experience, or important knowledge that could affect an investment decision.

They can also support each other in overcoming fears that prevent individuals from taking risks above their current comfort zone.

Some investment masterminds may choose to be specific (e.g. real estate), others more generic (e.g. any type of investment).

Personal Development

The world of personal development is pretty broad, so groups may choose to be very generic, while others have a more focused common goal.

Because of the common interest in self-improvement, group members can share resources or experience that can help other members, or simply get encouragement and support from one another.

Examples of goals may include reading a book every week, going to bed by a certain time, giving up alcohol, waking up earlier each day, meditating regularly, improving relationships, or developing a new skill such as learning a new language.

If you think about it, many support groups operate as a form of mastermind—anything from escaping domestic violence to overcoming addictions.

Many philosophers have also formed mastermind groups, as they provide an excellent platform for the development of ideas. Verbally expressing ideas and having other deep thinkers look for holes in their logic can lead to much stronger, more useful philosophies.

The possibilities are endless. Try joining or starting a mastermind to help you with your personal life goals, and experience the difference it can make.

Health & Fitness

From weight loss to body building, from overcoming chronic illness to competing in an Ironman, masterminds can help.

They give participants the ability to share in their collective experience, provide encouragement, share knowledge, and help one another maintain focus.

Masterminds are particularly useful in the health and fitness world for holding members accountable. It is easy to give up, especially when facing stressful periods of life.

Having other group members to answer to can dramatically increase the chances of you achieving your goals.

We will look at a variety of ways to really enhance the accountability effect in later chapters.

Writing and Other Creative Arts

Perhaps one of the most famous masterminds of all time was The Inklings. Its members included the likes of J.R.R. Tolkien and C.S. Lewis and helped produce works such as *The Lord of the Rings*, *The Hobbit*, and *The Chronicles of Narnia*.

Regular meetings ran for around sixteen years, and even after this they still met frequently for another fourteen years. Inklings claimed that the feedback they received from the group as their works progressed played a huge part in the quality of the final pieces.

Of course it is not just poets and writers that can benefit from a mastermind. Almost any type of artist, including playwrights, musicians, and painters, can improve their work when participating in a good-quality mastermind group.

Science and Innovation

Many inventors and scientists (including Thomas Edison and Albert Einstein) have also been part of a mastermind.

For scientists and inventors, getting a different perspective on a problem can be all they need to achieve a breakthrough.

Typically only one or two individuals will get all the credit for a new idea or achievement, yet almost always the end result was only achieved thanks to external input from a group.

Even the brightest minds become so much brighter when they are around other people who can think at a similar level. When scientists and inventors can set aside their ego and work collaboratively, they achieve so much more.

World Problems

The world is full of challenges. Environmental, financial, social, and political issues surround us. For those who want to address these issues, a mastermind can be the perfect structure to find solutions.

Take, for example, Sir Richard Branson's founding of The Elders, arguably one of his greatest achievements. The Elders are some of the world's wisest and most influential individuals, and they meet twice a year. Their objective is to find solutions to some of the world's most pressing problems and then help action those ideas.

Many politicians have also given credit to their masterminds in helping them lead their country better. Theodore Roosevelt, Warren G. Harding, and Sir Winston Churchill, amongst many others.

Of course you don't need to be Richard Branson or Theodore Roosevelt to use the power of collective intelligence to make a difference in the world. You may consider creating a mastermind of local people to help find and action solutions to local community issues.

Other

I have listed some common uses for a mastermind group, but don't feel that you need to be limited to just these examples. So long as a mastermind has a common purpose and its members either collectively or individually have goals they can define and work toward, a mastermind structure can be effective.

[5] BENEFITS OF A MASTERMIND

"As you navigate through the rest of your life, be open to collaboration. Other people and other people's ideas are often better than your own. Find a group of people who challenge and inspire you, spend a lot of time with them, and it will change your life."

AMY POEHLER

We have already discussed a few of the benefits of joining a mastermind group. But let's get a deeper understanding of what you will get from joining one . . .

Clarity

One of the most common benefits members experience is increased clarity. This can be invaluable in achieving your goals and raising the bar of your potential.

By taking the time to explain your goals and objectives to a group of peers, you actually gain clarity for yourself.

If you are not yet 100 percent clear, chances are the other group members won't be clear either. They will force you to explain yourself better, which leads to a deeper understanding for them and you.

Focus

Entrepreneurs, especially, tend to be very ADHD and struggle to focus on one project or even one task long enough to complete it.

A peer group helps keep you on track and helps you recognize when you are drifting. It can be well worth joining a group for this benefit alone, and its impact should not be underestimated.

Feedback

Once other members understand what you want to achieve they can provide invaluable feedback and advice. Sometimes this is where having a group with members from outside your niche can be particularly useful.

Getting a range of perspectives at an early stage in the development of our goals can prove invaluable later on. They can help refine our ideas, give us greater confidence in what we are doing, or help us change direction to something better.

A good mastermind will also help highlight any dangerous assumptions that you may have made. This is especially true for the members who are not so familiar with your industry.

Getting advice from someone who has been there before or is treading the same path can be a life saver. It is said that a smart man learns from his mistakes, while a wise man learns from the mistakes of others. A mastermind gives you the opportunity to be wise.

Expanded Network

To a large degree, the success of any business relies on the quality of its network. And indeed one of the more hidden benefits from a mastermind comes in the form of the expanded network it provides.

Every member has their own network, and each is usually more than happy to share their contacts. This may include suppliers, advisors, accountants, potential affiliates or partners, distribution channels, or perhaps even customers.

Leveraging the contacts and personal introductions from other members can really accelerate your growth.

Resources

It is not just contacts. Members are likely to have access to a variety of other resources. These can include specific books or training, investment capital, or something more tangible such as software or equipment.

In a good mastermind group, members are willing to share their resources to help assist each other.

Accountability

Perhaps the most powerful element of a mastermind group is the accountability it provides.

I am a fairly self-disciplined individual. I have worked ten to sixteen hours/day, six to seven days a week for years, purely from my own self-motivation (and out of choice). Yet I still find I can achieve more when I participate in a mastermind.

It's not that I end up working work more hours, far from it. It is just that the hours I do work become more productive due to the feedback of the group. I also focus on the most important tasks that I may have been avoiding (thanks to the commitments I make to the group).

For anyone struggling with self-motivation, the accountability of a mastermind group can prove critical to their success.

Emotional Support

Another benefit that should not be underestimated is the emotional support and encouragement that such a group can provide.

Regardless of whether you are building a business empire or trying to lose weight, improve yourself as a person, or change the world, you will face speed bumps along the way. Occasionally you may just crash head-on into a brick wall.

Generally, friends or family may struggle to relate or empathize with your situation. A mastermind, however, provides you with a network of people who "get it."

Having these people there for you can make all the difference in your ability to get through the challenges. At the very least, it will make the journey a bit easier.

Higher Standards

Using positive peer pressure can also help us aim for a higher standard. Almost all of us are capable of more than we realize.

Having people who support and encourage the best in us can really help is in becoming better and more successful people.

Thinking Bigger

And my personal favorite . . . Thinking bigger. I love the power of a group to take ideas and expand them to the next level. It is amazing how often a small idea can escalate into something really big and exciting.

[6] WHY MASTERMINDS FAIL

"The rising top executive, entrepreneur, or CEO can benefit from a mastermind group, to the extent the other members have as much to offer as they are willing to take from this relationship."

DAN PENA

It is an unfortunate reality, as with most things in life, that the majority of mastermind groups do not deliver for their members as well as they could.

More often than not this is because they are poorly organized or fail to meet the expectations of their members.

The sad part is that members of an ineffective or failed group can become skeptical about the potential value of masterminds altogether.

And the really sad part is that usually the failure of a group could have been avoided by simply addressing a few key points.

In this chapter, we will identify the most common causes of a group failure. In following chapters, we will explore the solutions to each.

Weak Leadership

The first cause of an ineffective group is simply poor leadership. Every group needs a degree of leadership: someone to create the group, schedule the meetings, and ensure rules are set and followed.

Look for a group with clear leadership, or if creating one, then step up and understand your role as a leader.

A leader needs to be clear in his or her role and set a good example to others in the group. If the leader is disorganized, late to meetings, or contributes little to the group, then you can be sure this will affect the behavior of other members.

With that said, leadership should not be confused with dictatorship. In a good mastermind, all members are equal and have equal say. The role of leadership within a mastermind should be thought of as closer to that of a facilitator.

Undefined Group Objective

If a mastermind group is not clear in its purpose, then chances are it will not last long. The only way to increase the chance of survival is to find and define a clear direction—and fast.

Without a clear identity and intent, members will join with their own expectations and agendas. These will likely conflict with each other and end in disaster.

If the group as a whole is uncertain where it is going, then individuals are likely to feel their participation is a waste of time.

Low-Quality Group Members

Weak members can cause a mastermind to crash fast. The analogy that a team is only strong as its weakest link certainly appears to hold true here.

When forming or joining a group, the quality of the other group members is critical. Due to the small size of a mastermind group, each person makes a significant difference.

This is not to say you won't make mistakes in accepting the wrong members. Chances are almost every group at some point will allow in a weak or disruptive member. In this situation, you need to let them go fast.

I will give you some suggestions on how to make this process easier shortly, but as always, prevention is better than cure. To minimize the need to prune members, a strict acceptance process is recommended.

Bottom line, a mastermind can only be as good as the people who are in it.

Too Many Members

"The more, the merrier" does not apply to a mastermind. When a group grows too large, its energy and focus will become too dispersed.

Members no longer feel they are getting the attention they need, meetings drag on way too long, and it even becomes difficult for everyone to contribute.

Lack of Belief

This is one of the reasons it is important to have a clear purpose for the mastermind and to have high-quality members. Every person must believe wholeheartedly in the reason for the group's existence and in each of the other members.

If members fail to believe, then doubt will creep in. And doubt is a disease that can destroy goals and relationships before you even realize it has taken hold.

This is not to say that at times individuals may not experience some self-doubt. This is almost inevitable during trying times. However, this is where the support of the other members comes into play.

If members do not believe in the group, then they are also unlikely to be very committed or to give 100 percent to it. These are all sure ways to erode a mastermind's effectiveness and, if left untreated, its life expectancy.

No Structure

One of the most frequent complaints I hear from people who have joined (and then left) a mastermind is the lack of structure.

An effective mastermind is rarely an informal chat over a coffee between friends. It is usually a well-structured and well-organized meeting with clear objectives and rules.

You will find that without a proper structure, you will quickly lose high-quality group members. Also, by having a clear and rigid structure, you will put off many lower-quality prospects from even applying to join in the first place.

One rule, in particular, appears to be important. That is the need for all members to attend every meeting unless there is a real emergency or exceptional circumstance.

Without this level of commitment, leadership is undermined, and the group can quickly fragment.

Poor Accountability

Accountability is one of the major benefits to a mastermind group. It is also one of the keys to keeping one alive and ensuring that you have only high-quality members.

A lack of accountability in the group can lead to members arriving late or not living up to their full potential. This can have a negative influence on other members, and so the group as a whole begins to fail.

In study after study, it has been shown that humans respond better to the stick than they do to the carrot. We often trick ourselves into thinking that the promise of reward is sufficient to create motivation. The truth is that the fear of loss is a much stronger driver for most.

This can be achieved through peer pressure (loss of respect), financial penalties (loss of money), or potential loss of membership to the group. For maximum results, I suggest a combination of each of these methods.

Members Fail to Grow Together

A recurring theme throughout this book is the importance of the group dynamic. If this is not built and maintained, then it can jeopardize the entire mastermind.

If one or two of the members accelerate way ahead of the others, or one or two fail to keep up with the growth curve of the other members, then the dynamic will be negatively impacted.

It is almost certain that each member will get their breaks and setbacks at different times, but over time, the average of each individual should grow in similar proportion to the others.

[7] FINDING AN EXISTING MASTERMIND

"The answer I found is you stay away from the people who make fun of you, and you join these ad hoc groups who understand your craziness."

RAY BRADBURY

A common challenge for many when they hear about mastermind groups is how to find one. The following is far from a complete list, but should be a good foundation for getting started.

Ask

It may sound obvious, but asking friends, family, and colleagues is often the best place to begin.

Many mastermind groups recruit through referrals, and an introduction can go a long way toward getting you accepted.

You may begin simply by asking around to see if anyone knows of a group that meets your needs. It is amazing how often what you are looking for is just around the corner, but until you ask, you never know about it.

You could also broadcast your request via e-mail, Twitter, Facebook, LinkedIn, or any other social network you are on. Just putting it out there can start a chain of events that will likely lead to success.

Google

Searching for something? Try Google.

Again, sounds obvious, but as they say, the obvious is easily overlooked.

Google has the ability to turn up threads on a variety of social media sites and forums that can often help you find existing groups or other people wanting to form a new mastermind.

Try searching for "mastermind group + your town/city name." Also try using the keywords for the type of mastermind (business, investment, writers, etc.) that you wish to join.

You may be surprised what lies just a short search away . . .

Meetup

Meetup.com has a wide range of groups, many of which are masterminds.

A quick search for the term "mastermind" and any associated keywords such as location and niche or focus type, and you will find a range of available choices.

These are usually free to join, and you can easily see how many members they have and how many times they have met and get an idea of how active they are.

The only issue with these groups is they tend to be larger and often less structured than the ones you will find through personal referrals.

Facebook

You can also try searching Facebook with the same type of keywords as used on Google or Meetup.

These groups tend to operate more like forums or large chat rooms than true masterminds. That said, there are some very valuable groups out there if you look.

Most of the high-end ones will be closed groups, so you will need to request access. Be sure to have your Facebook profile looking good before you do . . . you can be certain group owners will check this out before seriously considering you.

LinkedIn

A search for "mastermind" on LinkedIn produces hundreds of mastermind groups and thousands of individuals that list themselves as belonging to a mastermind.

LinkedIn is targeted at business professionals, so it is most suited to finding business- and investment-related masterminds.

As with any social media platform, public results tend to show the larger, less structured groups. But this can be a great place to start and to look for smaller or more local groups to join.

TheMastermind

TheMastermind.nz is a mastermind platform that enables users to create or participate in structured mastermind groups. These are usually small, focused groups and provide a much higher standard on average than many of the previous suggestions.

The platform enables you to search for groups that meet your specific requirements. It also allows you to see clearly what the group objectives are, who is currently a member, and how often the group meets.

As many of the groups use the platform to host their meetings, it means that mastermind members can be located anywhere in the world, so long as they have Internet.

It also includes an accountability system, helping groups to operate at a decent standard.

Regardless of the method or methods you use to search, don't be in a hurry to join the first group you find. Be sure once you find a group that they are a good fit for you and that you will be a good fit for them.

Only when you have found a good match will you truly gain value from the power of a mastermind.

[8] HOW TO BE A GOOD GROUP MEMBER

"Ants are good citizens; they place group interests first."

CLARENCE DAY

A mastermind group is much like a team. Every member needs to play well and work collectively for everyone to do well. This includes you.

As individuals, we need to take responsibility for our role in making any group we participate in a success. Here are just a few basic guidelines . . .

Give Before You Get

Aim to give more than you take. You may be there for your own benefit, but unless you contribute, you will soon find yourself unwelcome and find that others withhold their help to you.

Give your advice freely, share your contacts willingly, and offer assistance where you can. Do this, and you will find others will do the same in return.

No Pitching

You should also remember that a mastermind is not an appropriate place to try to promote your products or services. A common complaint is when one of the group begins shamelessly marketing themselves or their products.

Multilevel marketers are especially disliked for this. While some multilevel marketing training may suggest masterminds as a place to recruit, it is rarely appropriate to do so.

In a mastermind, you do not need to try to sell. Your business will get so much exposure to the group naturally that if anyone is interested, they will come to you directly after group meetings.

Good Time Management

Be respectful of everyone's time. Do not be that person who is always holding everyone else up.

Others may be too polite to say anything, but you can be sure most are frustrated by sloppy timekeeping. Arrive to meetings on time, and don't talk more than your allotted time.

On this point, don't hog the limelight either. This is something that is all too natural for some people.

In a mastermind, all members of the group should get roughly the same amount of time to talk and to give feedback. Learn to bite your tongue when others are talking, and be sure to give plenty of space for others to speak.

Be Humble

Learn to take feedback well. This is perhaps the hardest of all. Most people become defensive over their ideas, decisions or actions.

Remember, you are joining a mastermind to get honest feedback and ask other people's opinions.

Reality is you won't always like what they have to say. If you can't take feedback, then either people will stop giving it, or things may simply develop into a full-scale argument. Either way, this rapidly breaks down the effectiveness of a mastermind.

Take Action

Make an effort to achieve your goals. This, too, may sound obvious, but you will find many people don't actually try that hard. As a group member, though, it is not just yourself that is affected when you don't succeed.

The quality of the entire group suffers. If one member regularly fails to follow through with what they say they will do, then a negative feeling starts to build. Again, don't be that person.

Be Respectful

Be respectful of the group rules. I am not a big fan of rules in general. I have never been the type of person to fit in any box.

When it comes to masterminds, though, the rules are there for very good reason. Without them, the value of the group diminishes, and with no rules, the group often ceases to be effective at all.

[9] THE IMPORTANCE OF HARMONY

"Harmony makes small things grow, lack of it makes great things decay."

SALLUST

When Napoleon Hill first wrote about creating a mastermind in *The Law of Success*, he stressed the importance of harmony within a mastermind.

To understand why harmony is so important, let's take a deeper look at the meaning of the word.

Harmony is defined as "the state of being in agreement or concord."

Synonyms include concord, accord, agreement, peace, peacefulness, amity, amicability, friendship, fellowship, comradeship, solidarity, cooperation, understanding, consensus, unity, sympathy, rapport, goodwill, and like-mindedness.

As you read this list of synonyms, it becomes clear the type of group dynamic that is required for a successful mastermind.

That is not to say members cannot play devil's advocate with each other's ideas or don't give critical feedback. Indeed, this can be an extremely valuable part of the mastermind experience.

However, members do so in a caring way. And because of the harmony within the group, this type of feedback can be effective instead of being seen as negative or antagonistic.

It takes time to build this level of trust, acceptance, and cooperation within a group, and of course, you need the right personalities to begin with. However, once this harmony is established, then the real power of the group can begin to emerge.

As Sallust points out, lack of harmony results in decay, and so it is with a mastermind.

Should a group fail to develop harmony or should something happen to disrupt it, then corrective action must be taken immediately.

This may require acknowledgment and open discussion of the cause or even dismissal of a disruptive member of the group. Either way, until harmony is restored, the group's effectiveness will be severely compromised.

If you are joining or forming a group, look to ensure there will be no personality clashes and that members are there to work together in solidarity. All too often, people joining a mastermind do so for selfish reasons and behave in a selfish manner once in the group.

This selfish attitude is counter to the principles of harmony and must be eliminated for the group to reach its maximum potential.

Harmony also increases trust. Trust is another essential component within an effective mastermind. Without it, members will not feel confident to share openly or to fully participate.

Giving anything less than 100 percent will limit the value of the group for everyone.

If you find yourself as a member of a group that is inharmonious and nothing is being done to address the problem, then I would suggest leaving. Seek or form a new one.

Do not let a negative experience put you off. Learn from it and move on.

[10] CREATING A MASTERMIND

"If you have the opportunity to do amazing things in your life, I strongly encourage you to invite someone to join you."

SIMON SINEK

Another option if you can't find a mastermind that meets your needs is to create one.

There are plenty of people looking to join a mastermind; they just need someone else to take the initiative and kick things off.

The first thing you need to do is define the group's mission and purpose. What type of group is it? (Business, investment, personal development, social change, writers group, etc.)

What are the primary benefits you want members to get from participating? (Shared networks, feedback, help solving problems or developing ideas, accountability, etc.)

Write the answers to these questions down so you and future prospects can be clear as to why the group exists.

Once you have done this, you can then decide on the maximum number of members you want. Personally, I find about five to be optimal. This gives enough members to provide a solid range of advice, feedback, and contacts. It is also small enough that things don't get out of hand.

Really, three is the minimum you want, and ideally not more than six, seven at the very most.

Will your group be free or paid? Free makes it easier to attract members, but many people have found the quality and commitment of paid members to be higher (on average).

You could consider having all members donate a fixed amount to a charity each month. No donation, no membership. This gives the advantage of a paid membership while reducing resistance to the fee, and it makes all members feel more equal.

You will also need to decide on the frequency of meetings. This will depend on the type of group you are creating and the expected size of members' goals, how self-motivated they are, and everyone's location.

As mentioned, The Elders meet twice a year. This group, however, is made of very busy, highly achieved individuals, and collectively they are aiming at large social goals that take significant time to achieve.

Most groups benefit from meeting around twice a month. For others, weekly is more suitable, and for some, once a month is sufficient.

You may need to experiment a little to find what works best for your group.

Another consideration will be the length of sessions. Ideally, this should be no more than about one hour. Time is valuable, and you want to use it as efficiently as possible.

People's concentration begins to fail quickly in the high-intensity environment of a mastermind session. If sessions frequently drag on, members will soon become restless and eventually drop out.

The next step will be to draw up a clear list of rules. This sets expectations and standards for new members. For example:

- All members are expected to contribute to the group and assist other members when possible.
- Sessions start on time, no excuses.
- Members are expected to attend every session without excuse. Only in exceptional circumstances is absence acceptable.
- What is said during a mastermind group must remain confidential and not be repeated outside of the sessions without permission.
- No cell phones, social media, or other distractions allowed during meetings.
- All members are expected to put forth maximum effort in contributing to the group and in achieving the goals they set for themselves in the group.
- No member may use the group as a way to try to sell their products or services to other members.
- Lying about your actions or results in relation to goals set during

masterminds may result in membership being revoked.

- All members are expected to be polite and courteous to each other at all times.

For some, these type of rules may seem unnecessary, but you will find they go a long way toward enhancing the quality and effectiveness of the group.

Next you will need to decide on the structure and format of the group. We will look at the most common options shortly . . .

[11] NAMING YOUR MASTERMIND

"The beginning of wisdom is to call things by their proper name."

CONFUCIUS

There have been many famous masterminds throughout history, and all that I can think of had a name.

The Inklings, The Tennis Cabinet, The Junto, and The Vagabonds are perhaps some of the most famous examples. (An excellent article on these four masterminds can be found at www.artofmanliness.com/2010/12/01/iron-sharpens-iron-the-power-of-master-mind-groups/.)

As with any group or club, a name gives the members a collective identity. This creates a stronger sense of belonging amongst members and forms an entity that is separate from any one individual.

Any good marketer knows the power that lies in someone's sense of identity. Companies such as Apple have focused almost all of their marketing efforts on just this. Even religions have used it for thousands of years.

Another angle that many gurus use is to call their mastermind an "inner circle." This creates the impression of being intimate, trusted, included, and exclusive. It also creates the feeling that if you are not a part of the inner circle, then you are excluded. And no one likes to be excluded!

You should take time to give your mastermind a name, and take the time to make it a good one.

There are no real rules here, other than try to make it cool and interesting to the type of people you wish to join. Also aim to make it no more than one or two words (not including the "The").

If you can, try to create something that is easy to use when describing oneself.

For example, with The Vagabonds, it is easy to make the statement "I am a Vagabond," or with

The Inklings, you can easily make the statement "I am an Inkling."

Doing so will help members adopt part of the group identity within their personal identity. This will help strengthen the bond between members and therefore strengthen the group as a whole.

It will also help when recruiting members. Having a strong group identity builds the prospects' desire to be a part of that group (e.g., I really want to be an Inkling).

To enhance this identity effect even further, you may also create a group emblem and motto. Think secret society. Something that evokes emotion or a sense of purpose.

Essentially, branding a mastermind with a name, logo, and motto may feel unnecessary, but it is certainly worth the effort.

[12] STRUCTURING YOUR MASTERMIND

"I don't think that scheduling is uncreative. I think that structure is required for creativity."

TWYLA THARP

Deciding on the right structure and format of your mastermind is critical. Here we will examine some of the three most common structures, along with their pros and cons.

Freestyle

This is the way many groups operate. Basically, there is little format, and they are more a casual get-together to discuss a common subject and, often, to socialize.

This style is usually not suitable for web-based masterminds and instead is better suited to in-person meetings.

This type of structure (or lack of) can hold some value. It is a great way to allow spontaneous brainstorming over new ideas or as a way to learn more about each other.

However, value usually runs thin after just one or two meetings, and serious members who value their time drop out quickly.

It is hard to create any type of accountability, and dominant members of the group will usually grab most of the attention.

You may consider incorporating a freestyle meeting once or twice a year, but I would avoid making it the primary format for your group.

The Hot Seat

The hot seat method focuses on one or two members (depending on time) each meeting. The member in the "hot seat" gets the full attention for the entire session while the other members help brainstorm solutions to their problems.

This provides huge benefit to whoever is in the hot seat. The lengthy focus really allows the group to drill down deep and find solutions or create ideas for them.

Other members can gain benefit by listening to the ideas the group comes up with and then cross applying those same ideas to their own situation.

A good way to run a hot seat session is to have the person in the hot seat start by explaining their current situation, their goals, and their challenges as they see them. They can also explain any areas they would particularly like help with or any type of contacts they are looking to make.

During this process, members can ask questions to get more detail or help gain clarity, but feedback or comments are withheld. It can be useful to have one of the other members assigned to take bullet point notes on a whiteboard for reference later on.

In the next phase, the group then starts brainstorming ideas or solutions or providing information, resources, or contacts that may help that individual.

This can often help ideas expand way beyond the original concept. The hot seat method is a very powerful technique to growing those big ideas.

In the final phase, the hot seat member defines his or her goals and action steps. This will give them a clear idea of where they are going and how they will get there.

The main issue is that this format can become boring quickly for many of the members who are not in the hot seat. The motivation to attend meetings when it is not their turn is low, and the wait between hot seat sessions can be lengthy if the group is too large or meets infrequently.

Despite the huge value of this type of method, many groups that use it struggle to really keep traction because of the above-mentioned issues.

Those that do use this method successfully will often meet once a quarter and lock down for one to three full days. (This will depend on the size of the group and the length of time given to each member).

Doing it this way can be a great way to achieve some intense, retreat-like focus and can provide a boost throughout the year.

The Three Round Method

The three round method, on the other hand, uses a structure that gives each member an opportunity to contribute and benefit from every session.

It uses a similar process to the hot seat, only much more condensed.

In the first round, members review their progress since the last meeting. Did they achieve their goals, what challenges did they experience, and what were the results?

In the second round, each member has a turn to discuss their current challenges, objectives, and intended goals. Other members get to give feedback, ask questions to increase clarity, identify potential problems, offer advice, or share resources and contacts.

In the third and final round, members set their specific goals to be achieved and any specific actions they will take, usually by the next session.

One big benefit to this model is that each member gets to maintain momentum with each meeting. It also engages every member every time.

The more frequently a group meets, the more manageable the goals can become. While members may still have long-term goals, the short-term steps to getting there become much clearer, and support is provided along the way.

Perhaps the most powerful benefit, though, comes from the accountability of having to review your goals at every session. Sadly, without this, all of the great ideas that are created during a hot seat session will often end up a total waste of time.

The downside is that less time can be spent getting to the real nitty-gritty of one person's challenges or potential.

There is also the danger that meetings can drag on so that every member gets their turn. The alternative is for sessions to run out of time and some people are skipped. Without discipline, it can be all too easy for someone to hog the spotlight.

The Combination Approach

If you want to get the best of all worlds, then consider creating a combination of the previous methods. As a suggestion . . .

Every six months have a freestyle, informal get-together. This can allow members time to talk about anything they want, get to know each other on a more personal level, and allow the conversation to go where it wants.

Once every one to three months, use the hot seat method. This gives every member the chance to get some solid attention and get massive value from the group.

Then use the three rounds method two, three, or even four times a month. This ensures everyone gets a chance to keep moving forward, hold each other accountable, and fully participate.

If you decide to use a combination approach, then be sure to clearly structure it, so members know what to expect, when, and clearly explain to them why.

You can, of course, customize the suggestions here to best suit the size, structure, and nature of your mastermind. Each group will have its own optimal structure; it will be your job to find what best fits yours.

[13] RECRUITING FOR A MASTERMIND

"This, then, is the test we must set for ourselves; not to march alone but to march in such a way that others will wish to join us."

HUBERT H. HUMPHREY

Before you begin recruiting, make sure you have your group's purpose and objectives clearly defined, along with the structure of meetings and the benefits new members can expect to gain by joining.

This will help filter out anyone that may not be a good match and attract those who are.

To get your group kick-started, begin by thinking about people you already know that may be a good fit. Whatever you do, don't just recruit people because you know or like them.

Remember, the effectiveness of a mastermind is limited by the quality of its members. Asking someone to join only because you like them is never a good idea.

It can be a good idea to write out a detailed description of your perfect member. This is very much the same idea as when a product owner, marketer, or copywriter creates a customer avatar.

This avatar would include what type of person they are, their interests, spiritual or political beliefs, and personality traits such as loyalty, honesty, and reliability.

Ask yourself questions such as what is their education or level of experience? What are they looking to get from your group, and what would you like them to contribute?

Hopefully, you will know and like at least one or two people that would be perfect for the group. If so, great. Invite them.

If not, don't become desperate or in a hurry to fill places. Inviting the wrong people is a sure way to lose the right people fast. If you need more members, then it is time to start searching beyond your immediate network.

Often the best recruits come through a referral. To get referrals, you need to ask. Start by sending out a message to friends, family, and colleagues. Ask if they know of anyone suitable that they would be happy to recommend.

Don't assume that everyone understands what a mastermind is or what type of person would make a good referral. Make sure your referral requests include a clear definition of your group and its purpose, along with a profile of what type of person you are looking for. This will help save a lot of time and embarrassment rejecting people that were way off the mark.

You can also post your request on Facebook, Twitter, and LinkedIn, etc. Much like a job vacancy, the more people who apply, the better your odds are of getting really good applications.

If you are really struggling to find members or are very serious, you may also consider putting ads up on classified sites, on community notice boards, or even in the local paper.

Starting a post in a related forum or Facebook group is also another great way to find potential members. These are full of people with similar interests, so your chances of finding a member or two there are quite high.

If you have a mailing list that is relevant to your group, then consider e-mailing the people on that list an application form. Or if you are a blogger, create a blog post about your new group and include a link to apply.

If you are using a mastermind platform (such as www.TheMastermind.nz) to structure and run your mastermind group, then make sure your group is publically listed so people can search and find you.

You may want to start your own Meetup.com group too. This can be another way for people to search and find you.

There are thousands, if not millions, of people out there wanting to join a mastermind. If you set your mind to it and take the simple actions suggested here, you will have your group full in no time.

[14] FILTERING APPLICANTS

---

*"Great minds discuss ideas; average minds
discuss events; small minds discuss people."*

ELEANOR ROOSEVELT

I have said it before, and I will say it again: the
quality, effectiveness, and life expectancy of a
group is limited by the quality of its members.

That means you need to filter applications.

Consider applicants' background, personality,
achievements, education, and contacts. Check
their level of commitment to the group, and
ensure they are willing to contribute as much
as (if not more than) they expect to take.

Identify their suitability to the group. Find out
what they have to offer that will strengthen the
group dynamic. You can do this through a little
research and by asking them directly.

Many successful groups require an interview
process. If an applicant fails to show or does
not show on time, then you can probably
disqualify them immediately.

Also be sure to find out the reasons, objectives, and expectations of a prospective member. You may be surprised how much these differ from your own. Never make assumptions.

If you have existing members, then applicants should be reviewed and voted on by the rest of the group. It important that members get on well with and feel they have a choice in who they mastermind with.

Another way to filter applicants is to have a joining fee. This works well if you have some high-profile members or a solid reputation, but may be more difficult when first starting.

Another method uses a financial penalty to enhance accountability (which we will look at next). The penalty level also doubles as a filter, which ensures everyone is playing at a similar level.

[15] CREATING ACCOUNTABILITY

"Accountability breeds response-ability."

STEPHEN COVEY

Humans are masters of self-justification, excuse making, and denial. Even the super smart are usually just cleverer in the ways that they are able to deceive themselves.

Most of us are also incredibly good at overestimating our abilities and underestimating our time. It is perhaps for these reasons that we do not accomplish more with our lives.

Masterminds are great at helping create new ideas, which is great. Unfortunately, there is no such thing as a million-dollar idea, only million dollar results from enough of the right actions.

And this is where masterminds really pay off (when used correctly). They encourage and assist members in taking the actions needed that lead to the results they are after.

A good mastermind will not accept excuses. It will be brutally honest but in a kind and supportive way.

For accountability to work, members need to quantify what will happen before the next session. This can be broken down into two types of targets: either specific goals or clearly defined actions.

Goals are outcome orientated and will potentially require many actions to achieve. A goal may be to lose a specific amount of weight, to increase average monthly sales by 200 units, or to add $20,000 of assets to an investment portfolio.

Whatever the goal, it should be possible to measure the change. The person setting the goal should be able to show evidence that the goal was reached. This maybe through photos, screen capture, documents, or other tangible proof.

With clearly defined actions, on the other hand, there is no guarantee of outcome. The guarantee is only that the agreed action steps will be taken by the set date.

This may include calling X number of prospects, writing a document of a specific length, placing an advert, or completing a specific task.

Again, these goals need to be measurable, and where possible, look for ways to demonstrate evidence. This may not always be possible or practical; however, it really helps to stop members from lying to themselves (and to the group).

At each meeting, members must prove that they did what they said they were going to. Other members then vote on whether the goal was achieved to a satisfactory level or not.

For the best results, try to make voting anonymous. While some people are not worried about what others think, most are. By hiding votes, it prevents the group from influencing one another and helps make voting more honest.

The next step is to decide the consequences of failing to meet objectives. This may simply be group disapproval, which can be surprisingly powerful.

At the very minimum, though, I would suggest membership termination as the penalty if goals are regularly not met.

This helps create additional pressure for members to deliver on time. It also helps weed out those members who are not playing at a high enough standard and makes room for those who will.

Another strategy is to have members pay a fine if they don't take the actions or achieve the goals they set for themselves.

This can either be a set fine that is the same for all members of the group or a fine chosen by the member for each specific goal or action.

Personally, I prefer the standardized fine method. By having a set amount, it means that all group members are playing at the same level.

Whichever way you do it, it is important the penalty fee is high enough to be painful but low enough to be realistic. This, of course, will be a different amount for different people.

For one person, $5 may be sufficient; for another, $500 may not be emotionally motivating enough. It all depends on someone's personality and bank balance.

Especially for business- or investment-related masterminds, setting the penalty fee is a simple way to help determine the level of those participating. For example, a solo entrepreneur just starting out is unlikely to have the ability to pay a $1,000 fine, whereas a business owner making over seven figures a year should have no problem.

One question that always comes up is, what happens to the fine money? This is a tricky question, and ultimately you will need to decide.

Many groups decide to give the fine money to charity. While this may be good for society, it has the downside that it can actually decrease the effectiveness of having a financial penalty.

Remember I mentioned we are masters of self-justification?

Well, many people justify to themselves that if they don't reach their goals, then at least the money is going to a good cause. The whole point of the penalty is to feel bad, not to feel good.

Another option is to divide the money between group members. This can work okay, but there is the danger that it can create a bias toward deciding if another member should be fined or not. This is usually not a big issue but something to be careful of.

Actually giving the money to someone you don't really want to have it causes more emotional pain, and, therefore, is likely to be more effective. The most important thing is to create as much pain as possible and eliminate any feel-good factor regarding what happens to the fine money.

Another option is to get creative and have a little fun with the penalties. For example, they could be more embarrassing (in an acceptable way, of course) rather than financial.

You could create a list of "punishments" that are all pre-agreed on by members. These could include things like wearing their underwear on the outside of their clothes and going for a walk in public, or having to walk around a shopping mall backward while whistling.

An alternative type of punishment could be based around unenjoyable tasks. Ideas such as washing all other members' cars or cleaning their toilets. Basically something no one will want to do.

When one of your group fails to deliver, they must randomly select a punishment from a hat and then action that punishment before the next meeting. If they fail to do so, they lose their place in the mastermind.

Whichever form of accountability you choose, it needs to be enforced. Without enforcement, it ceases to be effective and undermines any other rules or procedures you may have.

[16] THE PIRANHA TANK METHOD

"Any time people come together in a meeting, we're not necessarily getting the best ideas; we're just getting the ideas of the best talkers."

SUSAN CAIN

The Piranha Tank was a mastermind group and structure devised by myself and Zach Grove. It combined the three rounds method with financial accountability and gave it a more rigid framework.

We found this to be particularly effective, so I will share it with you here. Feel free to copy or modify it if it helps you.

Our group was limited to a maximum of six members, though we usually had only five. Meetings were every two weeks. Members needed to own their own business and share the joint focus of accelerating their business growth.

Each member needed to put in a deposit before joining the group. This acted as security for any potential fine and quickly weeded out many unsuitable applicants. If a member ever left the group, they had their deposit refunded.

Meetings started at 7:00 p.m. sharp. If someone arrived a minute late or failed to show, they were fined the full amount of the deposit. This ensured full participation from all group members and avoided wasting anyone's time.

At the start of each session, one person was designated as the group facilitator. They then started and stopped each of the rounds using their phone as a timer.

The first round began with each member having two minutes to explain if they achieved their goals from the previous meeting and to prove it if possible. As soon as the two minutes were up, the focus shifted to the next person, and their two minutes began.

Once everyone had reviewed his or her progress, we moved to the second round. This involved each member being put in the spotlight and then having the other members share their thoughts and feedback.

The person in the spotlight got three minutes to explain their current situation and what they were trying to achieve and to ask for any specific feedback, help, or contacts they may need.

Next, each of the other members had just ninety seconds to offer their thoughts or help in some way. If they couldn't finish everything within that time, they could tell the person in the spotlight to contact them after the mastermind was finished.

Once every person gave their feedback, then it became the next person's turn to be in the spotlight. This continued until every member had their turn.

In the third and final round, each member got two minutes to list the goals and actions they would commit to achieving before the next session. By leaving this until the very end, it gave everyone time to digest the feedback given in round two.

If, during any of the rounds, a person finished everything they had to say before their time was up, then things simply moved straight to the next person.

If members failed to meet their goals, then the penalty was applied. If members did not want to lose their money, they always had the option to take their deposit back and leave the group.

This structure may sound very strict and fast paced, and it is. For five members all in attendance, the entire session usually lasted just one hour.

Round 1

Person	1	=	2	minutes
Person	2	=	2	minutes
Person	3	=	2	minutes
Person	4	=	2	minutes

Person 5 = 2 minutes

Total time = 10 minutes

Round 2

Person	in	spotlight	=	3	minutes
Person	1	feedback	=	1.5	minutes
Person	2	feedback	=	1.5	minutes
Person	3	feedback	=	1.5	minutes

Person 4 feedback = 1.5 minutes

Total for 1 person in the spotlight = 9 minutes

Total for 5 people in the spotlight = 5 x 9 = 45 minutes

Round 3

Person	1	=	2	minutes
Person	2	=	2	minutes
Person	3	=	2	minutes
Person	4	=	2	minutes

Person 5 = 2 minutes

Total time 10 minutes

All three rounds combined have a total of sixty-five minutes. Typically, not everyone takes their full amount of time on every round, so sessions finish within the hour.

You may think that such a short amount of time is not enough to achieve anything useful, but you would be wrong. It is amazing how much information people can share in such a short time when forced.

Usually, people waffle way too much. In this situation, they get straight to the gold. The trick is to ensure everyone abides by the rules and moves on when their time is up. This can require having a disciplined group and a firm session facilitator.

By using this technique, everyone gets equal attention. Quieter individuals who may have great ideas but are suppressed by more dominant members get to share their wisdom. No one is left out or left behind.

The strictness on penalties is understood by everyone to be for the benefit of all members. It is their choice to be there, and if they deliver as they promise, then no money is lost.

[17] THE FIRST SESSION

"Freaky things happen all the time in the world. I suppose everything has to happen for the first time at some point."

JOHN JEREMIAH SULLIVAN

The first meeting of your mastermind will be a little different than the ones after that.

You will need to lay the framework of what is to come, cover any group rules, collect penalty deposits if applicable, and, of course, get all the introductions out of the way.

Here is a general guide, just to help you get things off to as smooth of a start as possible.

1) Introduce yourself, what the purpose of the mastermind is, and why you decided to create the group.
2) Have each member spend just one minute each to introduce their name, where they come from, and what they do.

3) Explain the structure for future sessions. Make sure every member understands how things will be run and what to expect.

4) Cover the group rules. Make it clear from day one the standard at which you expect the group to operate.

5) Take any general questions at this point to make sure everyone is on the same page.

6) Have each member spend three to five minutes explaining more about themselves and, if relevant, their business. Have them answer the following questions:

- How did you find out about the mastermind, and have you ever participated in one before?
- What are the main benefits you hope to get from being in the group?
- What is your ninety-day goal?
- What is your twelve-month goal?
- What are your core skills and strengths?
- What are your biggest weaknesses, and where do you need the most help?

7) Check with everyone to see if there is any reason the proposed meeting times or schedule will pose a problem. Better to clear any issues now if possible.

8) If you plan to request deposits, then ask people to bring them to the next meeting. This will give anyone who is not happy with the group for any reason an easy way out. (Better to give weak members a simple way out now rather than have them making excuses later.)

9) If you need more members, then now is the time to ask the group if they would like to nominate a referral.

10) Take any final questions and wrap up the first meeting with a clear agreement as to when the next one will be and what to expect.

It can be a good idea to arrange an informal social drink or chat after the meeting so people can get to know each other a little better. To help avoid building bad habits, make this clearly separate from the main meeting. You may even want to make this in a different location.

The first meeting is important and will set the tone of things to come. That said, don't expect to get much immediate value from it. Removing this expectation from yourself and others will help take the pressure off.

Remember to relax and have fun.

[18] TIPS TO RUNNING THINGS WELL

"Be a yardstick of quality. Some people aren't used to an environment where excellence is expected."

STEVE JOBS

In all likelihood, if you are the one who creates the mastermind, then you will be the one who needs to run it.

If you want your efforts to be a success, then you will need to have clear rules and make sure members follow those rules. That said, try to structure things in such a way that the group operates and holds itself accountable as much as possible.

Discipline

If rules are broken, there needs to be a clear process that will, if severe enough or broken frequently enough, lead to loss of membership.

This may sound harsh, and certainly is not a good feeling, but it is critical to the effectiveness of the group.

One of the first things you need to become very disciplined with is punctuality. Time is our most precious resource, and it is essential that group members value each other's time.

No Excuses

To be really effective, excuses can't be tolerated. If weak excuses are accepted, then the group quickly starts losing its strength.

Blaming the weather, the traffic, your boss, your partner, or some other reason only gives away your power to do something about whatever was "stopping" you.

The word "blame" can be broken down to b-lame. When you choose to be lame, you cripple your ability to take action. It is each member's responsibility to plan their time more efficiently and make sure they arrive to meetings or complete tasks on time.

You will often find that certain people are always late and full of excuses, while others always manage to find a way to be on time regardless of how busy they are.

If people are unable to manage their time, then let them go. The A players in any group rarely tolerate excuse making, so if you want to surround yourself with A players, then you need to remove the excuses makers. Simple as that, and no excuse!

Now, occasionally someone will have a very good reason for not showing up, being late, or not delivering on their goals. For example, if they end up in a car accident on the way to the meeting, then that may be considered reason enough.

In the Piranha Tank, we would vote on whether we considered a reason to be acceptable enough to avoid penalty. Most often, though, members knew themselves, took responsibility, and paid the fine without a vote ever being needed.

Use Proper Tools

Another tip to doing anything, including running a mastermind, is to use the right tools for the job.

If you are organizing a group, then you may want to set up a private Facebook or Skype group for easy communication between members. Which network or platform will work best depends on your members. No point in setting something up on Facebook if half your members don't use it.

If you are conducting meetings remotely, then consider Skype or Hangouts, as both provide free group conferencing facilities. You can also use something like Google calendar to create a group calendar that can be shared between members to schedule meetings and send automatic reminders.

If you are timing meetings, then something like the Zazen Meditation Timer app can be an easy way to program the different rounds and session lengths. Once set up, this is much easier than using your phone's default timer.

The most dedicated option, though, is www.TheMastermind.nz, as this makes it easy to visually queue members automatically, has sessions preprogrammed, and helps take care of reminders and accountability.

When you use the right tools, structure becomes easy. This increases your chances of running things well, certainly makes it easier, and will increase the probability that your mastermind group will thrive.

Communicate Well and Often

Proper communication is key in any organization or relationship. A mastermind really is an organized relationship; therefore, it is doubly important.

Keep members updated on any changes, remind them of upcoming meetings, and ask for feedback, ideas, or suggestions for improving the group. Send out notifications that you think may be relevant or useful to group members.

There is, of course, a balance to this. Members don't want to be bombarded with junk or excessive notifications, but most mastermind hosts sit way too close to the lack of communication line.

Generally, an e-mail and/or text once or twice a week should be sufficient, with an additional monthly update or occasional feedback request.

On the topic of communication . . . If you see problems beginning to arise, perhaps someone turning up late often or friction between certain members, then address it sooner rather than later.

Dealing with problems before they escalate will be much easier and will help keep other members from feeling bad or being dragged into the bad feeling.

Take a Break

Yes, we all need a break once in a while. If meetings happen every week for years on end without a rest, people will burn out.

It is also common for many people to want to switch off or have some family time during certain public holidays. Respect this, and perhaps formalize it for everyone.

[19] THE FACILITATOR IS THE DETERMINING FACTOR FOR SUCCESS

"I believe that a good mastermind is like a secret weapon."

TIM CONLEY

As a high-level mastermind facilitator for many years, Tim Conley has learned through experience what is needed to manage a group.

This chapter is written by Tim himself to share his wisdom on how to run a successful mastermind:

In the last few years, I've run multiple masterminds. Not only have I made good money from this, but also the members of these groups have gone on to build game-changing businesses.

They've 10x-ed their revenue, disrupted stagnant industries, hired superstars, and changed their lives.

Running masterminds can be an excellent income stream. If you charge $500 to $1,000 per member per month, you will create a solid revenue stream from a few hours of work each week.

However, you must provide exceptional value in every call and focus exclusively on your members' businesses—not on improving your own.

Do not charge for profit if you are looking to extract value for yourself. That is not how it works. Only charge for profit if you are confident that you can create an exceptionally valuable environment for the members and that they will get more than their money's worth.

Humans do not do well without clear leadership.

This is particularly obvious in business settings; without a vision and clear guidelines, things get messy very quickly, and masterminds are no exception.

No mastermind will work without a designated facilitator. If you're the one who put the whole thing together, then this is your responsibility, and you must take it seriously.

To be a great facilitator, you must have some specific qualities and be prepared to do certain things that others will not:

- You must be focused and decisive.
- You must be willing to corral the conversation and steer it back to the topic at hand when people go off on tangents.
- You must be willing to call people out when they are not following through on their commitments.
- You must be willing to kick people out if they are not participating or refuse to play by the rules.
- You must be perceptive and be able to draw the best information out of people (by asking good questions and picking up on what's important).

As I mentioned above, you should not be looking to get value out of a mastermind that you are facilitating. If you need input on your business, join someone else's group.

However, if you have business acumen and are good at leading people, then running your own can be very rewarding.

If you are the facilitator, you should always be looking for fresh inspiration and information to take back to your group.

Maybe you're part of a forum or another mastermind and can pivot the information you collect there to benefit your members.

I've done this consistently over my years running masterminds, and leveraging external information can be very powerful.

A few more things you will need to be comfortable with as facilitator include the following:

- Keeping everyone on task and on time
- Starting and ending calls on time
- Managing the relationships within the group
- Paying close attention to the subtext or hidden meaning in conversations
- Taking deep dives into a topic or problem when needed

Finally, managing the members is a critical skill.

Not everyone will be a good fit for the group: people won't take it seriously enough to prepare for calls, will only contribute in so far as they expect to get value for themselves, or will miss calls or turn up late.

Some people will just be discordant: they'll make things too personal or will take things too personally. Some people will be mean in their delivery of criticism, disparaging of other members, or generally combative.

In that case, it's up to you to remove them.

You must always put the interest of the group ahead of any individual member.

If someone is creating problems, cut them quickly. Refund their money if need be, but always, always move quickly. Nothing kills a group faster than a destructive member.

The value of a good mastermind is hard to overstate. It draws the very best out of people, both in terms of creative, growth-focused ideas, and in how they relate to other entrepreneurs.

It allows you to connect people in a powerful, profitable way. Businesses go through drastic growth, and entrepreneurs hit the velocity they've dreamed of.

Focus your mastermind on providing world-class value to every member.

Pursue real engagement, and protect the group relentlessly from discord and apathy. Bring fresh inspiration and deep focus to every meeting.

If you can do these things, you'll watch your members become empowered and create unstoppable momentum in their businesses . . . and you'll get to be right at the center of it all.

Tim has been serving entrepreneurs as a marketer, mentor, and executive coach for over sixteen years. He is the creator of the Founder to Leader Transformation (FLT) Program where he trains entrepreneurs. You can listen to his daily entrepreneurship podcast at TIM411.com.

[20] HOW TO PROFIT FROM A MASTERMIND

"Profit is not the legitimate purpose of business. The legitimate purpose of business is to provide a product or service that people need and do it so well that it's profitable."

JAMES ROUSE

Many people start a mastermind simply to create something they wish to be a part of. For others, it is more a business model in and of itself.

However, it is suggested that if you run a mastermind for profit, then you put yourself in the role of organizer and facilitator only.

This means that you won't take the hot seat or spotlight yourself, or seek to directly benefit yourself from the group discussion. Doing so can create a conflict of interest and certainly creates inequality within the group.

This is not to say you won't find huge benefit from organizing such a group. It is likely you will still enjoy the expanded networking, stimulation of ideas, and the motivation a mastermind provides. You just won't get to discuss your goals personally.

Starting a paid mastermind is particularly easy if you already have a good reputation and a modest following in your chosen niche. However, there are ways to achieving this for anyone willing to put in the effort.

There are two simple ways of generating revenue: either have members pay a joining fee, or charge a monthly or annual membership fee.

The joining fee, of course, is rather limiting. Unless you have an unlimited group size, you will only make money when you recruit new members.

This leaves the monthly or annual options. Monthly gives a lower point of entry; annual offers greater security of revenue. You could, of course, also consider quarterly or bi-annual payments.

Some big-name gurus can charge upwards of $50,000/year for access to their mastermind. That is not bad for a side income. However, even a moderate level group can generate some respectable additional revenue. There is also no reason that you can't run more than one.

To justify any type of fee and especially to keep members paying it, you need to ensure the group provides genuine value. This will require structuring things well, being an effective leader, and providing value.

Work hard to ensure the quality of the group, and use a strict application process. This will help build a strong, worthwhile mastermind.

Remember, too, that many people join a mastermind because of who is in it. The profile of the person running it can be especially important.

This means if you don't already have a solid reputation, you will need to work on creating one for yourself. A quick and easy place to start is building a social media presence.

If you are building a professionally orientated mastermind, then LinkedIn is definitely the place to start. If it is more health and fitness orientated, then Facebook is probably the place to begin.

You want to brand yourself as an expert, so be sure to sell yourself on these platforms. Interact in forums and chat groups around your topic, and start increasing your visibility in the communities that hold your prospective members.

The better you brand yourself, the easier it will be to attract members to your group and the higher price you will be able to charge.

This is a book on running a mastermind, not branding. However, here are a few basic ideas to get you started. You will, of course, need to study any that interest you, in much more detail.

Writing a book can be a great way to create authority and get exposure to attract prospective members. This may sound like hard work, but it can be easier than most people realize, especially if you know your topic well.

Either hosting a podcast or becoming a guest on other people's podcasts is another way to gain authority and build a name for yourself. Try to focus on content or shows that are related to your topic. As a guest, you will want to work your way up the podcast ladder.

Start with small shows that are struggling to find guests, and begin there. It will be easy to get an interview, and you will have the chance to build confidence and refine your presentation. From there, work your way up the podcast ladder to the larger shows with bigger audiences and more credibility.

You can use the same approach with guest blogging. Many blogs are looking for additional content, so this can be a great way to get yourself in front of targeted audiences and establish your reputation.

No matter which strategies you use, you will, of course, want to find a way to pull the listeners onto a mailing list. From there, you can further build a relationship and begin to market your mastermind to them.

[21] ADDING VALUE

"People who add value to others do so intentionally. I say that because to add value, leaders must give of themselves, and that rarely occurs by accident."

JOHN C. MAXWELL

Try to give your group additional value by going beyond just a standard mastermind structure. This is especially important if you are charging for membership.

Here are just a few ideas to get you started . . .

Guest Speaker

Perhaps once every one to three months, bring in a guest speaker to present on a specific topic. This may be accounting, legal, or marketing for a business group, or perhaps an NLP practitioner or life coach for a personal development group.

Some speakers will be willing do this as a way to get additional exposure; others may require a small fee. Chances are your group will already know many suitable people who will happily speak as a personal favor.

By creating focus sessions around a particular topic, members can fine-tune their skills and bring a greater degree of awareness to a specific area of their life or their business.

Speakers are usually open to answering questions. This can be extremely valuable to members, as they can get specific information directly from an expert for free.

Members Sharing

Have a time set aside at each meeting for members to share some new insight, wisdom, or skills they may have. This could be just five or ten minutes at the end of each meeting.

This is valuable in two ways: both to the group and to the person sharing.

Members will get to learn new skills or gain insights in a concentrated form. The person sharing gets to challenge themselves, improve presentation skills, and build self-esteem.

Resources Area

Making a shared resource area for members to reference and contribute to can be a great way to add easy value.

You can create a hidden web page or a shared Dropbox folder with links to trusted sites, services or consultants, etc. You could also share other resources such as books, training, or other relevant content such as checklists and content summaries.

Online Group Chat

Having someone you can turn to for advice when you need it can be very valuable.

In the Piranha Tank, we used a private Facebook group, but you could just as easily create a skype chat group or use any other group messaging service.

We found that it was a great way to bounce ideas off each other or get feedback on progress between meetings.

Members never abused this opportunity and kept its use to important requests only. Everyone was happy to support each other, and it made a significant contribution to the overall benefit of belonging to the group.

Social Events

If it is practical, consider organizing regular social get-togethers for group members, and perhaps their families.

This not only helps provide additional value, but it also helps establish stronger bonds between members.

Members get to learn more about each other, chat casually, and strengthen social ties that will enhance the group dynamic during meetings.

Even if your members are spread around the country or the globe, consider trying to meet once every year or two. These in-person meetings together will do more to strengthen friendships than months of masterminding alone.

Inspirational Quote

Okay, I know this is overdone a lot, but I for one still love hearing new nuggets of wisdom or being reminded of old ones.

Quotes provide aha moments for people, which trigger a feel-good response in the brain.

If you can associate that connection to your mastermind, this can only be a good thing.

Often a well-timed, well-phrased quote is all that is needed to inspire us or lift us through a difficult period. This makes them ideal to incorporate as part of your meeting schedule.

As a group facilitator, make it your role to find a new quote for each session, or have members take turns sharing their latest favorite quote. Either way, it costs nothing, takes almost no time, and people love them.

Provide Notes and/or Recordings

If you are a group host or facilitator, consider recording meetings and making the recordings available to everyone afterward.

You could also have the recordings transcribed or bullet pointed for members. If you are good at note taking, you could simply take shorthand notes and then write them up after meetings.

Either way, this provides a record of agreed goals, gems of wisdom, and those million-dollar ideas. It also allows members to focus fully during sessions.

[22] THE ULTIMATE MASTERMIND

"Courage means to keep working a relationship, to continue seeking solutions to difficult problems, and to stay focused during stressful periods."

DENIS WAITLEY

It is said that behind the success of every great man is a great woman. And many successful women, too, have claimed the support of their partner invaluable in their achievements.

While there are many exceptions to the rule, it is certainly true that a lot less in this world would have gotten done without many couples forming masterminds in their relationships.

This is not to say that every romantic relationship forms a mastermind. Far from it. Let's remind ourselves what constitutes a mastermind . . .

A powerful mastermind is made of two or more people working together in harmony to achieve a similar or same outcome.

A relationship certainly is made of two people, but, unfortunately, they don't always share the same (or at least similar) goals, and sadly, they are not always harmonious.

If a couple is to maximize their individual potentials, then they need to learn to realize their collective potential. That is, they need to make their relationship their primary mastermind.

To do this, they must be clear in their collective goals and ensure they are in alignment with each other. They must seek to support one another and to avoid placing blame on the other person.

They must work in harmony to solve the inevitable challenges that will arise throughout the course of their lives. They must also learn to hold each other accountable and to give feedback without being judgmental. And of course, they must trust and respect each other.

Such a romantic partnership may be one of the easiest masterminds to start, but perhaps the most difficult to main and grow.

However, if a couple is able to achieve this, it will likely be the most rewarding thing they ever do. It will also provide the backbone for all their other collective and individual achievements.

Napoleon Hill also pointed to the romantic mastermind as being the most powerful. He believes it was the foundation to Henry Ford's success. Without his wife's support and encouragement, his participation in the more famous Vagabonds mastermind may never have occurred.

Reread the chapter on "The Importance of Harmony," and apply the principles to a loving relationship. This is perhaps the cornerstone of a successful marriage or life partnership.

A productive relationship cannot exist if either or both of the partners subconsciously sees themselves in competition with the other.

As with a sports team, co-operation and putting the team before the individual is the only way the team will win. It is also the way the individual players get ahead, too.

It is easy to understand that when everyone pushes in the same direction, then it is easier to travel further with less effort. If there is too much fighting, then energy and time are wasted. The journey becomes hard work, and progress is slow.

I began this book with a quote from Henry Ford, and I am going to end it with another. This is perhaps the most profound, important, yet simple philosophy to making relationships (personal or professional) a success. It is this:

"Don't find fault, find a remedy."

[23] AFTERTHOUGHTS

"It is the mark of a good action that it appears inevitable in retrospect."

ROBERT LOUIS STEVENSON

Over the years, I have been as guilty as many writers and entrepreneurs of trying to do too much alone. And over the years, I have realized what a mistake this is.

However, it was not until I wrote this book that I came to realize the importance that masterminds (both formal and informal) have played in my development.

I have always considered them important (otherwise, I would not have even begun writing this in the first place). However, as I look back, I can see how critical masterminds have been on so many levels. There is no way I would be where I am today without them.

The power of a small group of focused, likeminded individuals is perhaps the most underrated force on the planet. If you have a desire to create or change anything, then this is the place to begin.

Too many people spend too much time thinking "one day." I beg you, don't be one of them.

Do not underestimate the difference you can make in your own life, the lives of your family, and in helping overcome the planet's problems—big or small. The sooner you start, the bigger difference you will make.

Many great personal development and business books have stressed the importance of purpose, clarity, visualization, focus, action, and persistence. Unfortunately, not enough have stressed how these will only take you so far.

Many great minds working alone only achieved mediocracy. Many mediocre minds working together have achieved greatness.

Masterminds provide the missing puzzle piece. And like most things, the more conscious you are of using them, the more effective they will be.

If you are ready for change, then take action today and make an effort to join or start a mastermind.

In the wise words of a little green Jedi, "Do or do not. There is no try."

APPENDIX 1: QUESTIONS TO HELP DEFINE YOUR MASTERMIND GROUP

1) What is the type of group you are creating? (business, investment, personal development, etc.)
2) What is the name of your group?
3) What is your emblem or motto (if any)?
4) What format/s do you plan to use? (freestyle, hot seat method, three rounds method, piranha tank, or custom)
5) How often do you plan to meet?
6) What time will you meet and for how long?
7) What is the maximum number of members you will accept? (5–6 recommended)
8) What benefits can members expect from joining?
9) What is the unifying purpose that members must share? (e.g. "To accelerate their business growth," "to take their investment portfolio from six

to seven figures," or "to lose weight using health strategies")

10) What are the specific requirements for joining? (Age range, gender, financial status, education level, location, weight, years of experience, etc. These should, of course, be relevant to your group.)

11) What tools will you use to help you run your group? (Google Calendar, Skype, TheMastermind.nz)

12) Is there a joining or annual fee? If so how much?

13) What will your application process be?

14) How will you recruit members?

15) What are your group rules?

16) What methods of accountability will you use?

17) If you are using financial penalties, how much will the penalty be, and when will it be applied?

APPENDIX 2: EXAMPLE OF A MASTERMIND STRUCTURE

It can be a good idea to have a copy of the structure you plan to use for both your own and other members' clarity.

Make sure your structure clarifies whose turn it is to speak, what the purpose of that section is, and how long it should last.

The following example uses the Piranha Tank structure as discussed in an earlier chapter.

Round 1: Review goals from the previous meeting. What did each member do? What were the challenges and results?

Person	1	=	2	minutes
Person	2	=	2	minutes
Person	3	=	2	minutes
Person	4	=	2	minutes

Person 5 = 2 minutes

Round 2: Spotlight session. Current focus and intended objectives of each member, along with feedback from the rest of the group.

Person	in	spotlight	=	3	minutes
First	person	feedback	=	1.5	minutes
Second	person	feedback	=	1.5	minutes
Third	person	feedback	=	1.5	minutes

Fourth person feedback = 1.5 minutes

This is then repeated until each member of the mastermind has had their turn in the spotlight.

Round 3: Specify quantifiable goals and action steps to be achieved by the next meeting.

Person	1	=	2	minutes
Person	2	=	2	minutes
Person	3	=	2	minutes
Person	4	=	2	minutes

Person 5 = 2 minutes

APPENDIX 3: EXAMPLE RULES SHEET

1) All members shall participate fully and make their best effort to attend every meeting.
2) Sessions start on time. Any member arriving even a minute late will be fined the group penalty fee.
3) Cell phones, e-mail, social media, TVs, and any other form of potential interruption or distraction must be closed or switched off during meetings. One hundred percent focus is expected.
4) Members will be polite and courteous to one another.
5) Members may not use the group for the promotion of their products, services, or opportunities to other members.
6) All information shared between members is strictly confidential. Any break of this confidentiality will lead to immediate termination from the group.
7) Meetings will follow the structure as laid out in the group structure document. Members will follow the

guidelines and be respectful of any time limits (and so not waste other members' time).

8) Any failure to achieve a set goal or take a specified action by a chosen date will result in the group penalty fee unless the group votes that your reason for not managing to do so is acceptable.

9) If you are unable to attend a group meeting, then you must notify the group organizer at the earliest possible time. Reasons must be considered and voted as acceptable by the group to avoid the penalty fee being applied.

10) At any time you incur the penalty fee, you may have the option to not pay and to leave the group.

APPENDIX 4: EXAMPLE RECRUITMENT INVITE

Business Mastermind Looking For New Members

We are a small group (max 5) of business owners who meet twice a month (Mondays at 7:00 p.m.) to help accelerate our business growth. Every member's business must generate over $500,000/year in revenue.

Benefits to joining the group include greater networking, honest feedback, help with problem solving, support in achieving your goals, and a strong accountability framework to help keep each other on track.

Applicants must be willing to help other members, open to feedback, dedicated to their goals, fully committed to the group, and be a solution-orientated individual.

For more information or an application form, please contact Your Name at Your Number or Your E-mail.

APPENDIX 5: SUGGESTED ACTION STEPS TO RECRUIT NEW MEMBERS

Recommended action plan to recruit new members:

1) Create your clear outline, purpose, and group rules for prospective members to see.

2) Create a short recruitment invite covering the core of the group's purpose, the benefits to someone becoming a member, and the time/frequency of meetings. Also include a short description of the type of person you wish to join.

3) Make a list of everyone you know, and try to filter it for those you think will be a good fit and might be interested in your new group.

4) Contact the above short list via phone or e-mail.

5) E-mail everyone you know asking them for referrals. Be sure to include a copy

of the recruitment invite and explain the type of person you are looking for.

6) Post your recruitment invite on any social media profiles you may have (Facebook, LinkedIn, etc.)

7) If you have any related mailing lists, then mail your invite to these lists.

8) Search Google for related groups and forums. Join them and participate a little before posting your invite there, too.

9) Post your invite to classifieds sites such as Craigslist or even on your local community notice board.

10) Setup a Meetup.com account and post your group.

11) If you are using TheMastermind.nz, make sure your group is set to public.

APPENDIX 6: EXAMPLE APPLICATION FORM

Name:

Address:

Phone number:

E-mail address:

Skype ID:

How did you find out about this group?

Current business or businesses. Please include age and basic description of each business:

Have you been a member of a mastermind group before? If so, please explain your experience and why you left:

What do you hope to gain from becoming a member of this group?

What do you feel you can contribute to the group?

What are your long-term business goals?

On which social media sites or other websites can we find out more about you, who you are, and what you do? (Please list URLs here.)

APPENDIX 7: STEP BY STEP GUIDE TO USING THEMASTERMIND.NZ PLATFORM

1) Create your account at www.TheMastermind.nz.
2) Click the Create New Group option
3) Follow the steps. This will help you define your group and set up scheduling.
4) If you would like other users to be able to find and request to join your group, make sure you have your group set to public.
5) Share the URL you will be given to invite new members from your existing networks.
6) If you are still short on members, follow the action steps in Appendix 5.

www.ingramcontent.com/pod-product-compliance
Lightning Source LLC
Chambersburg PA
CBHW070321190526
45169CB00005B/1696